TALKING TO GOD

God Bless

Delia Tombleson

ILLUSTRATED BY
Diane Matthes

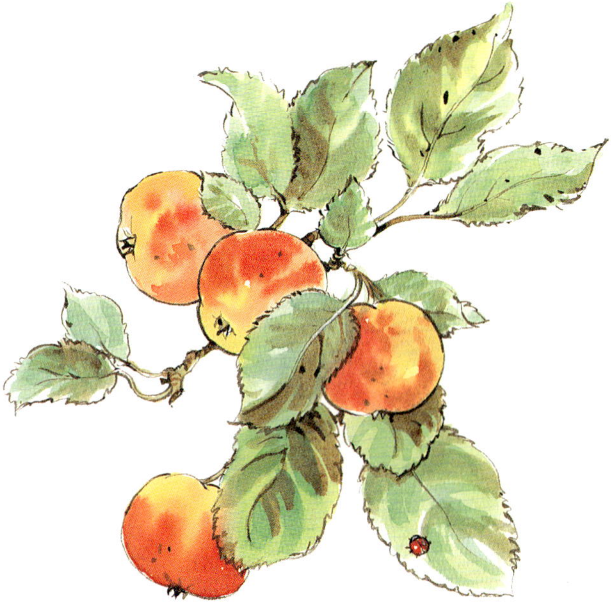

God bless us every morning
When the world is fresh and new,

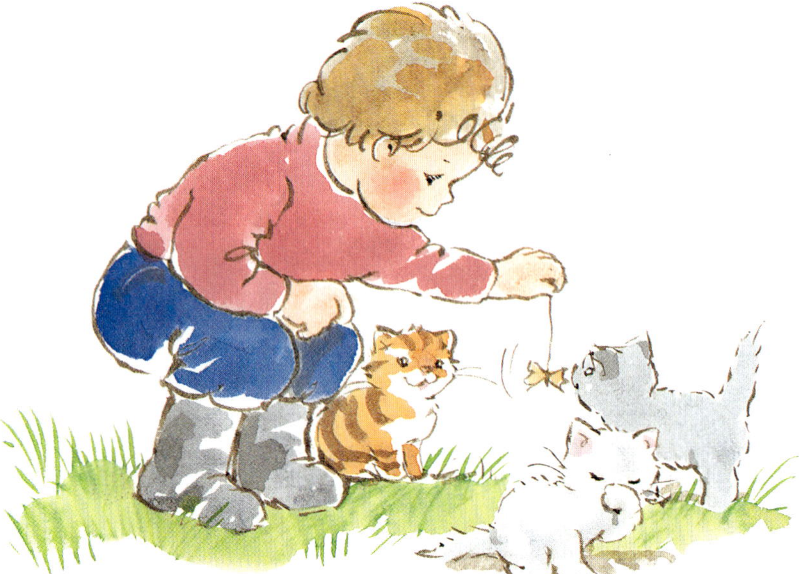

God bless us all the long day
In our work, and playtime too.

God bless us when we're sick
And cannot run and play,

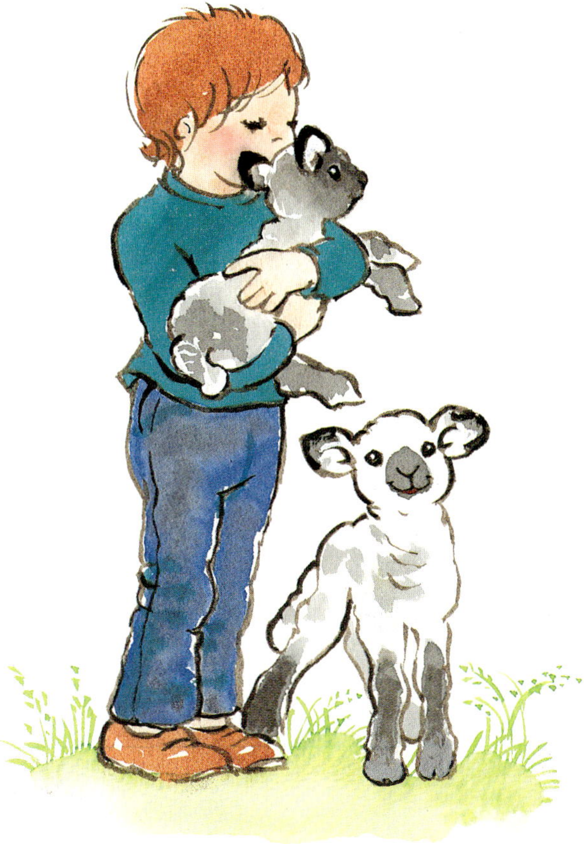

God bless the people who
Look after us each day.

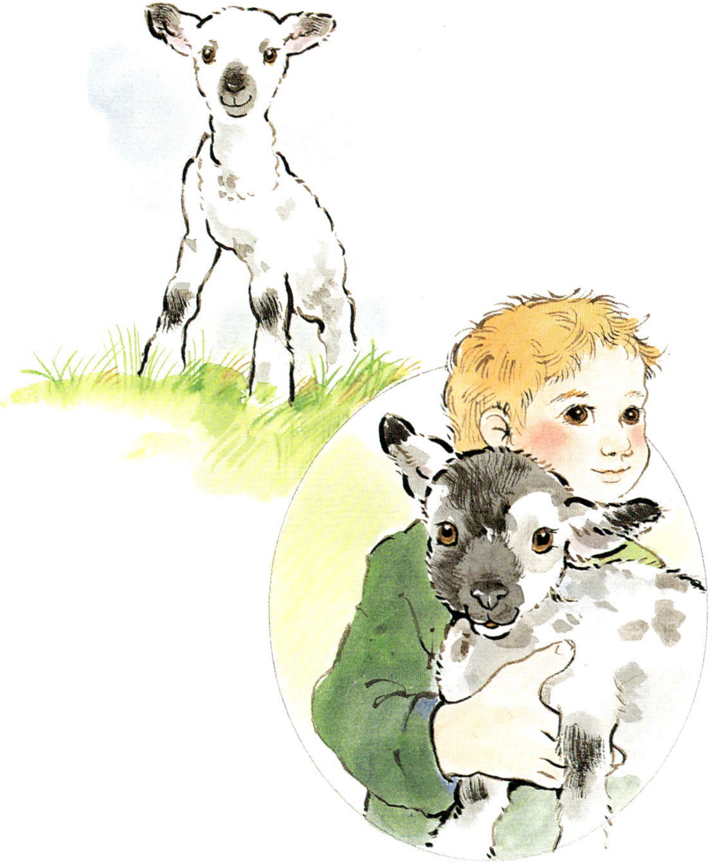

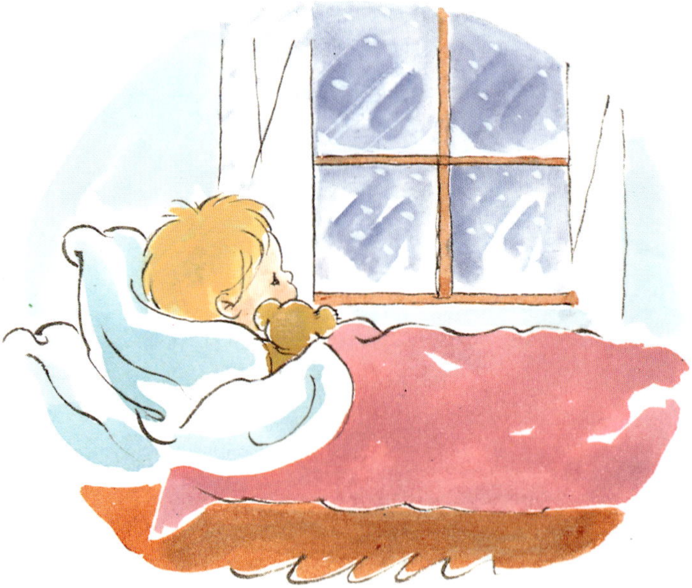

God bless us at the end of day
Saying 'goodbye' to friends,

God bless our fun with Mum and Dad
As another day ends.

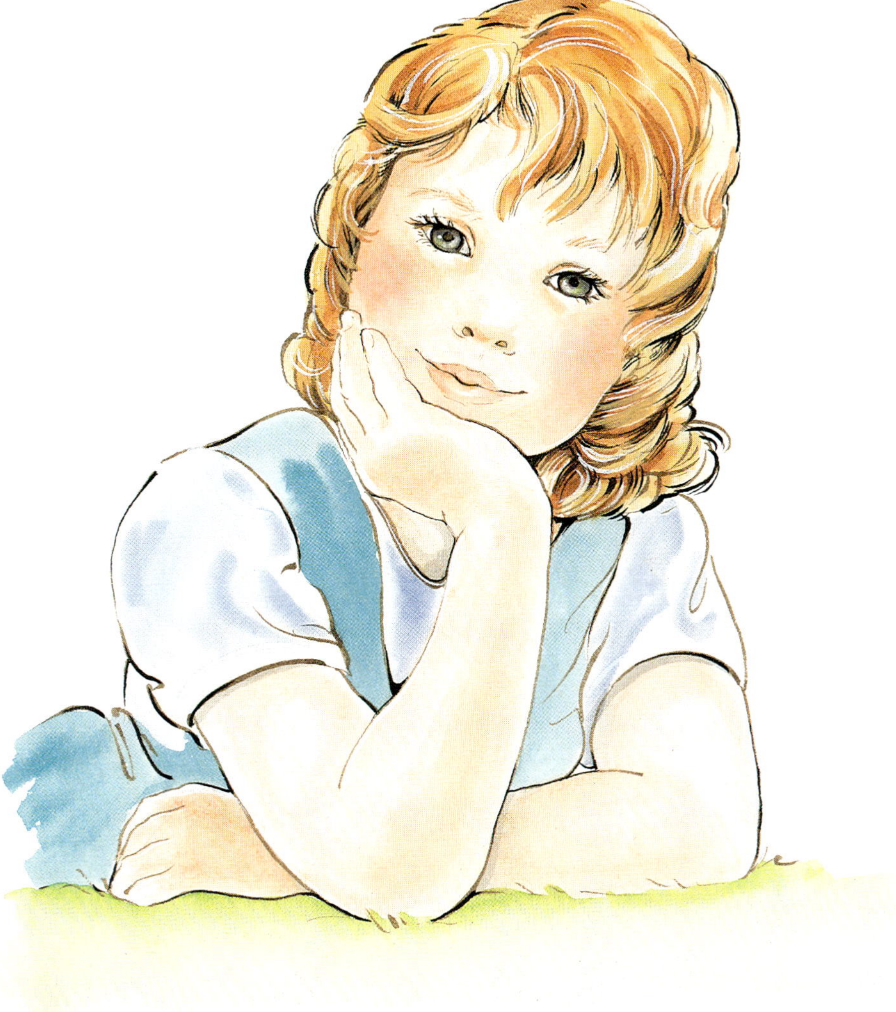

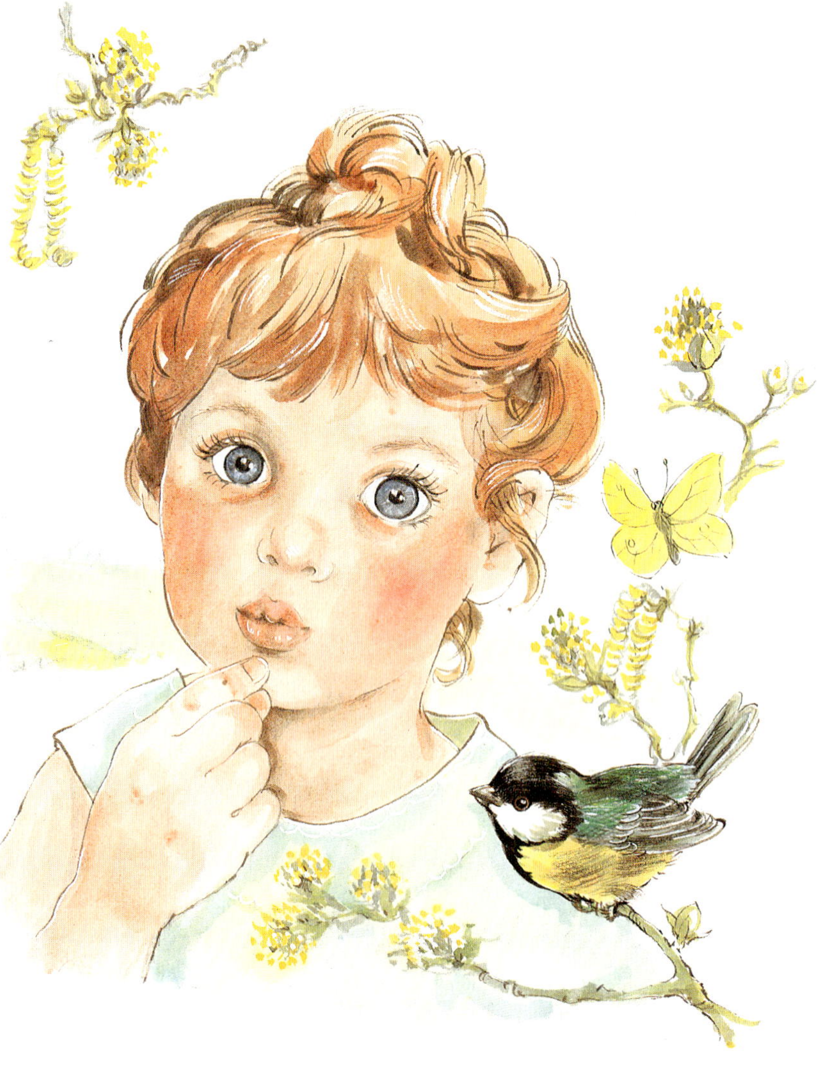

God bless the people we remember
In our bedtime prayers,

18

God bless the children without toys
Or food or clothes to wear.

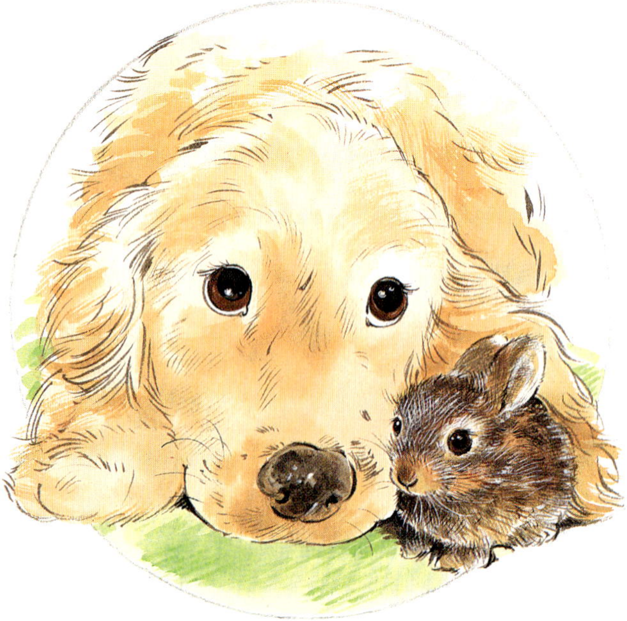

God bless us as we go to sleep
And make us quiet and calm,

God bless us all, through Jesus' love,
And keep us safe from harm.